# The Journey from Brokenness to Wholeness

## Overcoming the Life-Quakes And Storms of Life

By

**ANDRE THOMAS**

GREATNESS
PUBLISHING

Cover Design and Formatting by Farouk J. Roberts,
Brands & Love Creative
http://www.brandsnlove.com

Library and Archives Canada ISBN
978-1927579039

All Scripture quotations are from the New King James Version of the Bible, except otherwise stated.

www.greatnesspublishing.org

# Dedication

This book was finished because my wife Nina created an environment for my greatness to emerge.
I dedicate this book to her and our everlasting love.

# Acknowledgements

I wish to thank
my wife Nina; you are a great manifestation of God's favor
and faithfulness in my life.

Thanks to Farouk Roberts for the cover design and
formatting.

Thanks also to Valentine Dantes who contributed to the
final product with his editing skill.

A big thank you to the Holy Spirit, who anointed me to
finish this project. You are more than enough.

# Table of Contents

# Introduction

*He healeth the broken in heart, and bindeth up their wounds (Psalm 147:3).*

*I am forgotten as a dead man out of mind: I am like a broken vessel (Psalm 31:12).*

Man is a trinity. He is a spirit, has a soul and lives in a mobile home called a body. The body can be broken, the soul can be broken and the spirit can be broken.

King David eloquently described the impact of a broken spirit in a person, when he said, *"I am like a broken vessel" (Psalms 31:12).* Broken vessels leak out their contents. When a person's "heart" (another word for spirit) and soul are broken, that person "leaks" out their hopes, dreams, motivation, energy, anointing, courage, self-control and ends up depleted. Even love that others deposit in their lives may be received, but eventually leaks out.

Many have endeavored to find a cure for a broken heart. They have sought medication and have only found temporal relief.

Medication cannot solve the "leak," or fill the "hole" in the human soul.

Some have tried recreational drugs to create an artificial high and a sudden rush of pleasure, but this in itself proves futile, because drugs and alcohol cannot repair the damage and plug the leak in a human soul.

Some have turned to sexual pleasure and have found its temporal high to be ineffective in healing their broken hearts.

Others have sought to find relief in friendships, only to discover that a friend's love cannot heal their heart. They receive love but it leaks out. They are like a broken vessel. However, there is a cure for the broken heart and it comes from heaven above.

In Psalm 147:3, the Lord announces Himself and introduces Himself as the One who is able to heal the broken heart and bind its wounds. Only He is able because He is the manufacturer of the human soul. He stood in the garden and breathed into Adam, and Adam became a living soul.

On earth, there isn't a prudent inventor who will create a product he can't fix. Our precious heavenly Father is no exception. I declare to those who are broken :

There is an antidote that comes from heaven above for your brokenness.

I believe that these pages will impart the wisdom, life and healing you require for your restoration to wholeness.

David said in *Psalm 23, "He restoreth my soul."* The word restore means to bring back into a state of newness.

Your soul may have been battered, broken, shattered and fragmented by the storms and earthquakes of your life, but I declare by the Spirit of God:

Your days of secret pain and secret tears are ending, and wholeness is arising in you as the sun of righteousness rises upon your life with healing in his wings:

*"But unto you that fear my name shall the sun of righteousness arise with healing in its wings; and ye shall go forth, and grow up as calves of the stall" (Malachi 4:2).*

Understanding is the master key that unlocks wholeness. It is impossible to win a battle you do not understand. It is impossible to overcome a struggle you do not understand. *In Luke 11:52 we read: "Woe unto you, lawyers, for ye have taken away the key of knowledge: ye entered not in yourselves, and them that were entering in ye hindered."* Scriptural insights are the keys that unlock prisons for men and women held in Satan's bondage and open the treasure house of heaven in their lives.

I have therefore included questions for you to answer about yourself in this workbook. As you answer these questions, you will gain understanding of the nature of your brokenness and the appropriate scriptural solution will emerge.

Remember this: you may be in prison, but God possesses the keys to every prison.

Jesus, when He rose from the dead said, *"I am He that liveth, and was dead; and, behold, I am alive for evermore, Amen; and have the keys of hell and of death"* (Revelations 1:18).

I will share with you scriptural keys for unlocking the prison of emotional, sexual and relationship bondage in which many find themselves. I pray that through the pages of this book, God's wisdom will hand these keys to you. As you read and meditate on these words, may you have an encounter with Jesus, the healer of the brokenhearted.

# Chapter 1

## Understanding Brokenness

*And there was delivered unto Him the book of the prophet Esaias. And when He had opened the book, He found the place where it was written, 'The Spirit of the Lord is upon me, because He hath anointed me to preach the Gospel to the poor; He hath sent me to heal the brokenhearted, to preach deliverance to the captives, and recovering of sight to the blind, to set at liberty them that are bruised. To preach the acceptable year of the Lord (Luke 4:17 19).*

*Hope put off makes the heart sick, but desire fulfilled is a tree of life (Proverbs 13:12).*

*Reproach hath broken my heart; and I am full of heaviness: and I looked for some to take pity, but there was none; and for comforters, but I found none (Psalm 69:20).*

*...my days are past, my purposes are broken off, even the thoughts of my heart (Job 17:11).*

Jesus Christ our Lord, during His earthly ministry paid special attention to the condition of a broken heart. He said that the Spirit of the Lord was upon Him to anoint Him to bring healing to the broken hearted.

A broken heart, according to Scripture, is caused primarily by three things:

1. A Satanic encounter
2. The destruction of hopes and dreams
3. Reproach and disgrace

A broken heart is very similar to a broken bone.

Your soul consists of your mind, will and emotions, and when it's broken, your emotions become disjointed. Since your emotions determine how you feel, your feelings become disjointed as well. Your mind fragments and you develop a double or triple, or quadruple mind!

What does the Scripture mean by a double mind?

When people experience trauma, they usually process their trauma by putting it "on the back burner," or in the back of their mind, and act like it never happened. That's a form of survival. If the wound caused by the trauma is not healed, the person lives a seemingly normal life until an incident triggers the memory of the trauma. When this occurs, the person manifests the emotions of the trauma and not an emotional response that reflects the situation.

Here's how a heart can become broken:

**1. Satanic Encounter**

Job eloquently described the effect of a satanic encounter when he said, "...*my days are past, my purposes are broken off, even the thoughts of my heart*" (Job 17:11). The satanic encounter in the book of Job describes an attack of Satan that destroyed Job's family, wealth and health. This traumatic experience resulted in a broken heart.

The human heart lives on the oxygen of hope and dreams, and when the fulfillment of dreams are destroyed by demonic attack, man's mind and emotions become broken. There are many people reading this book who are facing the same condition that Job faced. Some of whom may have been raped, molested or stripped of their wealth or health as an evil wind from the devil came against the boat of their lives. Job did not remain in that condition forever because the Lord God, His Maker, repaired his broken heart and gave him back what he had lost:

And Jehovah turned the captivity of Job when he prayed for his friends. Also Jehovah added to Job all that had been his, to double.

*And came to him all his brothers, and all his sisters, and all those who had known him before. And they ate bread with him in his house, and consoled him and comforted him over all the evil that Jehovah had brought on him. Each one also gave him a piece of money, and each one a ring of gold.*

*And Jehovah blessed the latter days of Job more than the beginning. For he had fourteen thousand sheep, and six thousand camels, and a thousand yoke of oxen, and a thousand she asses. He also had seven sons and three daughters. And he called the name of the first, Jemima; and the name of the second, Keziah; and the name of the third, Keren- happuch. And in all the land there were not found women as beautiful as the daughters of Job. And their father gave them inheritance among their brothers. After this Job lived a hundred and forty years, and he saw his sons, and his sons' sons, four generations. And Job died, being old and full of days (Job 42:10-17).*

In these verses you can see that the Lord "turned the captivity of Job." But the Lord is the same today, yesterday and forever. Therefore, I declare:

The hour for your captivity to be turned has come.

## 2.  The Failure to Realize Hopes and Dreams

According to *Proverbs 13:12,* "*Hope put off makes the heart sick, but desire fulfilled is a tree of life.*"

Humankind is not infallible and when people fail each other, hope is deferred. What is hope? It is a passionate clear expectation of a good future. When your expectations for friendships, business relationships, marriage or parental love are deferred, your heart becomes sick. The word disappointment literally means, "The sad emotion felt when you miss an appointment with your desire."

The good news is, you can rise from that place and survive the disappointment. Your Creator anticipated that people will fail people and provided a way of escape. Paul said by the Holy Spirit, *"But my God shall supply all your need according to His riches in glory by Christ Jesus"* *(Philippians 4:19)*. You don't have to remain disappointed forever.

I declare that:

> An anointing from God's throne is coming right now to heal you from the disappointment of broken expectations.

Your need includes healing. Let me explain what that means.
Before car manufacturers release their product to the public, they create hundreds of warehouses with thousands of spare parts for every part in the car. Before you bought your car, the spare parts were already in place in anticipation that your car may become damaged. That's man's wisdom. God's wisdom is greater.

Our Creator anticipated your agony and struggles, and has prepared warehouses full of resources that you need.

Receive your miracle now!

## 3. Shame and Reproach

Reproach strips a person of dignity. It causes men and women, boys and girls to bow their heads. It could be caused by poverty. It could be caused by private or public humiliation. Those who have experienced it know how real it is.

David, in describing his reproach said, *"Reproach hath broken my heart; and I am full of heaviness: and I looked for some to take pity, but there was none; and for comforters, but I found none"* (Psalm, 69:20).

Heaviness or depression can be a product of reproach. It weighs down the human spirit and causes men and women to retreat and hide. Reproach has a tendency to inflict people with a mental virus that I call, "The victim virus." It's the "Woe is me" syndrome – the "nobody knows the trouble I've-seen" syndrome. But this syndrome is not your portion. You do not have to stay a victim forever.

There is an answer and a promise in Scripture for you: *"For your shame you will have double; and for disgrace they will rejoice in their portion; therefore in their own land they will possess double; everlasting joy will be theirs"* (Isaiah 61:7).

Our precious heavenly Father compensates those who have been reproached. Your God is able and willing to reverse your reproach and give you double compensation for your trouble! I declare that:

The anointing for your divine compensation is coming upon you now!

But there is a price to be paid for wholeness. Jesus, in speaking to a man with an affliction said, "Will thou be made whole?" It is a price of movement, understanding, faith and obedience to His instructions.

I urge you:

> Come out of the prison house of depression and sorrow.

I declare that:

> An anointing for your freedom is coming upon you now!

> Arise from your affliction, and with understanding, faith and obedience, lay hold of your antidote from heaven!

## PERSONAL APPLICATION

The problem that you cannot identify is the problem you cannot fix. I want you to identify areas of brokenness in each category of your life (if there are any) and what caused them.

Satanic Encounter

_____

_____

_____

_____

## The Failure to Realize Hopes and Dreams

_____

_____

_____

_____

## Shame and Reproach

_____

_____

_____

_____

_____

# Chapter 2

## My Personal Journey

I can write bout brokenness to wholeness because I have a mandate from God to set people free from bondage. The Holy Spirit has showed me concepts and principles on how to be free from the silent agony of a broken heart I have also applied the principles he gave in my life to be set free from d 5 seasons of brokenness.

I will share four with you.

1. The first occurred from my birth when a stammering infirmity stopped by ability to communicate my thoughts, ideas and insights to others. This affliction caused unbelievable pain as I battled thoughts of depression that gripped my life. I was gloriously healed at the age of 19 and was later healed of the emotional damage that affliction caused in my life.

2. The second occurred when my father disinherited me and threw me out of the house for obeying the call to preach. He was a leading intellectual in the country and wanted me to follow that path. This wounded me deeply and laid the foundation for my third season of brokenness. I was later healed from the experience and restored my relationship with my father.

The third occurred when I was a young man at age 21, who had lost his sense of connection with his father. That's when I made a marriage mistake and married a woman with similar wounds and hurts. I lived with her for many years and pursued the call of God on my life. Our union produced two wonderful children but after many years of marriage, we had a divorce, which caused unimaginable pain in my life. God later healed me from the experience.

3. The fourth was slander and character assassination. .It began because I made a mistake in entering a business and financial relationship with a man who did not share my values. When I ended the relationship, he began spreading half-truths and lies about me. Though I could have focused on blaming him for the damage caused, he was only doing what he knew to do at the time. I trusted the wrong person but thank God, I have been healed from the experience.

You can also be healed from every experience of brokenness regardless of whether it was caused by the devil, other people of your wrong choices. I am living proof!

# Chapter 3

## The Effect of Demons on People who are Broken

*A merry heart maketh a cheerful countenance: but by sorrow of the heart the spirit is broken (Proverbs 15:13).*

One of the most deadly and feared diseases among humanity is called AIDS or Acquired Immune Deficiency Syndrome. AIDS is an immune deficiency disease, which stops your immune system from working. It shuts down your God-given resistance to disease. People who have full-blown AIDS could die from a common cold.

There is a parallel in the emotional realm that the Holy Spirit has shown me. I call it **EIDS**– *Emotional Immune Deficiency Syndrome*. When a person's emotions are broken, their resistance to devils is significantly weakened. Let me give you an example.

I once had a staff member who was rejected by her father, abandoned by her mother and raped by her stepfather. For the purpose of this book, I will call her Susan. Now Susan loved the Lord, but because of her history of trauma she developed EIDS.

EIDS had two primary effects on her life:

**1. Her resistance to the spirit of rejection was very weak.**

Demons are very strategic and tend to attack people in their areas of trauma just like viruses and germs exploit weak immune systems. The spirit of rejection attached itself to her and in an attempt to compensate for it, she looked for love in all the wrong places. That opened her up to spirits of sexual addiction.

**2. She developed oversensitivity to simple situations that shouldn't normally cause pain.**

If your fingers were broken, a handshake from your best friend could bring you so much pain that you could easily faint. It is the same with broken emotions. When well-meaning, loving and precious people interact with the areas of pain in your life, they trigger the emotions of the trauma.

There were times when I saw Susan in church and didn't have the time to speak to her because I was concentrating on other matters. A person without her history would have understood that, but because of her broken emotions she felt rejected. Simple actions can cause great pain when people are physically, emotionally and mentally broken. Demons know this and prey on the emotionally wounded.

To judge Susan as simply an immoral woman would have been wrong. She needed wholeness, and when it came, the sexual addiction disappeared and the spirit of rejection took wings and flew away never to return again.
If you are suffering from EIDS, this can be your story too. You can be healed.

I don't know what demons have taken advantage of your lack of emotional and mental resistance, but I do know this: Jehovah Rapha, the Lord our Healer is able to restore your emotional immune system.

An understanding of the EIDS principle can help loved ones deal with people who have experienced trauma. After a person has experienced severe mental or emotional trauma, they need to be surrounded by a great deal of love as they try to regain and build up their emotional and mental immune system. Love is a shield and buffer against demons when they seek to infiltrate.


**PERSONAL APPLICATION**

What demons through (emotional problems) have attacked you in your state of Emotional Immune Deficiency Syndrome (EIDS)?

_____

_____

_____

_____

_____

State whether you have successfully won the warfare or whether you continue in struggles.

_____

_____

_____

_____

_____

# Chapter 4

## How People Compensate for Unhealed Brokenness

*I am troubled; I am bowed down greatly; I go mourning all the day long. For my loins are filled with a loathsome disease: and there is no soundness in my flesh. I am feeble and sore broken: I have roared by reason of the disquietness of my heart (Psalm 38: 6-8).*

Just like with physical pain, people with emotional pain reach for relief. Pain is a sign of disorder.

It is an alarm bell given to us by God to signify that something is wrong. We all know that innately. Not having the ability to feel pain puts you at a significant disadvantage in life. If someone didn't feel physical pain he or she could accidentally lean on a stove and get burned without feeling it. You could also have a life-threatening condition in your body and not feel the warning signs.

Pain triggers an awareness that tells you when something is wrong so that you can do what it takes to eliminate the cause. Similarly, emotional pain is not to be celebrated. Instead it points to the root of a problem that God can fix with your cooperation.

Those who don't know God's pathway to emotional and mental wholeness after life's storms and earthquakes have ravaged us, will always seek relief, even if temporary. That's natural. I don't judge them. I've been in that boat.

It's natural to seek pain relief.

People compensate for emotional pain in five basic ways:

1. Retreat and hide the pain
2. Seek intense pleasure to compensate for the pain temporarily
3. Ensure that others experience some of the pain
4. Seek to control everything and everyone so they experience less pain
5. Seek love in the wrong places in an attempt to heal the pain

## 1. Retreat and Hide the Pain

This reaction is easy to understand. If you fall and scrape the skin of your elbow, normally you would cover it with a bandage because it's unsightly.

In the same way, people "cover" their pain because pain isn't attractive. They hide their pain because they don't want to remember it. But the pain is ever-present and rises up like a ghost of the past.

People who choose this mode of compensation most often produce the fruit of alienation, insecurity, worthlessness and inferiority. If this is you, don't condemn yourself. I declare that:

The Lord your God is rescuing you from this bondage now and setting you in your place of destiny.

He wipes away your secret tears and gives you beauty for ashes because He comforts those who mourn in Zion.

*To appoint unto them that mourn in Zion, to give unto them beauty for ashes, the oil of joy for mourning, the garment of praise "for the spirit of heaviness; that they might be called trees of righteousness, the planting of the Lord, that He might be glorified" (Isaiah 61:3).*

## 2. Seek Intense Pleasure to Temporarily Compensate for the Pain

Others choose to counteract pain with intense pleasure. Hebrews speaks about the pleasure of sin: *"By faith Moses, when he was come to years, refused to be called the son of Pharaoh's daughter; choosing rather to suffer affliction with the people of God, than to enjoy the pleasures of sin for a season" (Hebrews 11:24-25).*

Certain sins, such as sexual sins and drug and alcohol addictions, create temporal pleasure. They give a high that causes the emotionally broken to temporarily forget the pain.

As people seek higher and deeper experiences with these substances to compensate for emotional pain, they become addicted. Some have become pleasure junkies who seek ecstasy even if it's only for the next five seconds. If this is you, don't condemn yourself. There is an antidote.

Now that you know better, choose the pleasures at the Lord's right hand which last forever: *"Thou wilt shew me the path of life: in thy presence is fullness of joy; at thy right hand there are pleasures for evermore"* (Psalm 16:11). I declare that

God's presence is coming upon you right now to deliver you from the bondage of the sin that medicated your pain and to lift you into the joy of His presence.

## 3. Ensure that Others Experience Some of the Pain

Proverbs 3:31 says, "Envy thou not the oppressor, and choose none of his ways."

Some choose to oppress others in the way they were oppressed. This is normally manifested through violence and intimidation. Take, for example, one of America's most notorious male serial killers. While he was in jail men raped him. He reacted violently to the trauma. After his release he captured other men, killed them, chopped them in pieces and put the pieces in a fridge.

This may seem like an extreme example but millions of people carry out a lesser form of reprisal against innocent people for the trauma they may endure over the course of a regular day. They have a bad day at work and make sure everybody shares the pain of their bad day. If this is you, I declare that:

> The Spirit of the Lord has come to bring liberty and set you free now from that bondage. Arise in the Lord! Cast off the lifestyle of violence and intimidation. Lay down the instruments with which you inflict pain and forgive your oppressors so that your sins maybe forgiven too.

## 4. Seek to Control Everything and Everyone so they Experience Less Pain

There are two types of control: positive control and negative control. Through positive control, a person controls things for which they are responsible and accountable. Through negative control however, a person attempts to control things for which they are not responsible or accountable. Negative control seeks to control what is none of its business!

Emotional pain can give birth to fear, which can also give birth to negative control. The greatest negative controllers in the world are simply broken people who are, with the help of demons, are seeking to control others so they can avoid pain themselves and compensate for fear. This mode of compensation is irrational and these people live in a realm where their broken emotions often hijack their intellect and common sense.

If this is you, I declare that:

> The Lord your God is here to deliver you from fear right now! God has not given you a spirit of fear but of power, of love and of a sound mind!

## 5. Seeking Love in the Wrong Places in an Attempt to Heal the Pain

Love is emotional food and drink but when you are hungry and thirsty for love, your judgment can sometimes be severely impaired.

I once had an associate Pastor, Happy Akasie, who shared an experience he had while traveling to the Sahara Desert. He and his traveling companions had taken containers of water to drink along the way. However, they had not anticipated that the extreme desert heat would cause severe dehydration, and they finished their water before they reached their destination. He and his companions realized that failure to drink additional water could cause them to pass out. He stated that their desperation for water caused them to see mirages – pictures of water in the desert that are not real, but are the product of one's imagination and burning desire.

Finally they saw some goat's drinking water from a filthy, dirty and stinking pool. They were so excited and happy that they saw the water as deliverance from God. They chased the goats from the pool and drank the filthy, dirty and stinking water to their hearts' content. They filled every container they had and happily and joyfully drank the water along the way.

I asked him if in his present state he would consider drinking such water again. He promptly said, "No!" Why? Because he was not in the same state of desperation.

This parallel is true in the emotional realm. The love-thirsty see love where love does not exist, just like Pastor Happy who saw mirages of water where water did not exist. They also gobble down perverted, stinking and filthy love from people thinking they are blessed. If this is you, I declare that:

You are about to have an encounter with Jesus, the Bridegroom the true Lover of your soul. Today, He is touching you and healing you wherever you hurt.

He is bringing you into a season of the most majestic and glorious love relationship with Him that you have ever had in your life.

## PERSONAL APPLICATION

Be honest with yourself and state how you compensate for your unhealed brokenness.

_____

_____

_____

_____

_____

_____

_____

# Chapter 5

## Things Brokenness Cannot Damage

Brokenness, though deadly, is not all-powerful. It cannot damage God's love for you. Scripture declares through Paul, *"For I am persuaded, that neither death, nor life, nor angels, nor principalities, nor powers, nor things present, nor things to come, nor height, nor depth, nor any other creature, shall be able to separate us from the love of God, which is in Christ Jesus our Lord"* (Romans 8:39).

As you hold and read this book, God's love is reaching and touching you. Brokenness cannot strip you of your worth and intrinsic value. We read in *Psalm 8:5, "For you have made him a little lower than God, and have crowned him with glory and honor."* This Scripture says that you personally have been crowned with glory and honor. You are like a 25 cent coin that fell on the highway. Rain came and beat it. Snow came and covered it. Cars came and ran over it. A garbage truck spilled garbage on it. But a young boy found it and took it to the bank. The 25 cent coin was still worth its original value of 25 cents.

What has happened to you cannot obliterate your intrinsic heavenly value.

The gifts and calling of God are without repentance (see Romans 11:29) and your pain cannot sabotage them. The devil cannot obliterate them and man's rejection cannot strip them off you. If you recognize this to be true, a fountain of faith will erupt within you and the prison doors will fling open before your eyes. You will walk out of your tomb of pain and will be resurrected just like Lazarus into a brand new day.

Jesus your Lord and Savior is the resurrection and the life, and you are never too dead for a resurrection.

You have a purpose from God. Discover it! You have a glorious destiny. Arise to it!

You have wonderful gifts in you. Manifest them!

There are people on earth waiting for the solution you can bring to their problems.
Find them!

## PERSONAL APPLICATION

What do you perceive is your God-given purpose?

_____

_____

_____

_____

_____

What do you perceive are your God-given gifts?

_____

_____

_____

_____

_____

# Chapter 6

## Love Tanks

Man is a spirit, has a soul and lives in a body. A man's soul consists of a mind, will and emotions. He comes in two models: a male version and a female version.

The body feeds on cooked plants and animals. The mind feeds on knowledge. The spirit feeds on the Word of God and drinks God's Spirit in God's presence.

The emotions feed on love.

Emotions determine how you feel. When they are not strong, your self-esteem (another word that describes your feelings) swings like a pendulum from positive to negative.

What makes emotions strong?

When a child is born, it is fed physical food which causes its body to grow. A child is also fed mental food called knowledge which causes its mind to grow. However, if a child is not fed love, its emotions will not grow or become robust and strong.

Every person should ideally receive four types of love before they get to age twenty. The fifth type of love is optional. I am going to describe the emotional containers of love as love "tanks" or love "containers."

1. The first type of love is called, "**I am Special Love**." This love is given to a child from birth to age seven. At this age, children focus on the authority and care figures to learn about themselves. They use them as mirrors of significance. If the authority and care figures reflect that they are valuable and treasured, they will internalize it and believe they are valuable and precious. If on the other hand, they neglect or abuse them, they will internalize it and believe they are worthless and irrelevant.

2. The second type of love is called, "**I Belong Love**." This love is deposited between the ages of 7 and 13 and is bestowed by peers of a similar age group. A child with a tank full of this love knows that other children love, accept and celebrate their person. A child empty of this love feels alienated, isolated and rejected.

3. The third type of love is called, "**I am Significant Love.**" This love is experienced by children from ages 13 to 18 as they start to understand and position themselves in the world. This love is related to a sense of consciousness that says, "I can achieve something significant in this world," and it's given by parents, authority figures and friends who speak words and demonstrate actions that affirm and crystallize the child's potentially significant contribution in the world.

4. The fourth type of love is called, "**I am Wanted Love**." This love is given to young persons from ages of 16 to 19. It communicates to the individual that members of society find them desirable. It is given as the young person experiences the wider world and is bestowed by parents, authority figures and mentors.

5. The fifth type of love is called, "**Self Love.**" This love is what a young person feels as they cross to adulthood from the ages of 19 through 21. It tends to set the foundation of their self- esteem during adult life. If the deposits of I am Special Love, I Belong Love, I am Significant Love and I am Wanted Love are low, the love that they give themselves will also be low. If they are high, their Self Love tends to be high. When Self Love is low, struggles with self-esteem and self-image become the pattern irrespective of external success. When Self Love is high, self-esteem is high regardless of external success.

Success cannot cure low Self Love. No amount of clothes, cars, tattoos and body piercings can fix it. It's like a bank account. When the money in it is low, it's low. When it's in the red, it's in the red. To those whose tanks are low on love, there's an antidote. It is called divine destiny love.

Divine destiny is the path and destination of glory, honor, value and the relevance that God has pre-determined for you. It requires your pursuit, understanding, faith and obedience to discover and walk in it.

This destiny distinguishes you and makes you special. It makes room for you in life and positions you where you belong. It positions you where you are celebrated and not tolerated. It causes you to offer a significant contribution and service to the lives of people and it comes with majestic destiny relationships with people that will celebrate your value.

A living consciousness of this destiny and your pursuit of it, will fill up any empty love tank. If you don't know your divine destiny, make it the most important pursuit of your life. ( *For more information on this subject read my book Discovering Me*)

The greatest day in your life is the day you were born.
The second greatest day of your life is the day you make Jesus Christ the Lord of your life. The third greatest day of your life, is the day you discover why you were born.

## PERSONAL APPLICATION

On a scale of 1 to 10 state the level of "I am Special Love" you received as a child.

| Low | 1 | 2 | 3 | 4 | 5 | 6 | 7 | 8 | 9 | 10 | High |
|-----|---|---|---|---|---|---|---|---|---|----|------|

On a scale of 1 to 10 state the level of "I Belong Love" you received as a child.

| Low | 1 | 2 | 3 | 4 | 5 | 6 | 7 | 8 | 9 | 10 | High |
|-----|---|---|---|---|---|---|---|---|---|----|------|

On a scale of 1 to 10 state the level of "I am Significant Love" you received as a child.

| Low | 1 | 2 | 3 | 4 | 5 | 6 | 7 | 8 | 9 | 10 | High |
|-----|---|---|---|---|---|---|---|---|---|----|------|

On a scale of 1 to 10 state the level of "I am Wanted Love" you received as a child.

| Low | 1 | 2 | 3 | 4 | 5 | 6 | 7 | 8 | 9 | 10 | High |
|-----|---|---|---|---|---|---|---|---|---|----|------|

On the scale of 1 to 10 state the level of your "Self Love."

| Low | 1 | 2 | 3 | 4 | 5 | 6 | 7 | 8 | 9 | 10 | High |
|-----|---|---|---|---|---|---|---|---|---|----|------|

On the scale of 1 to 10 state the level to which you are walking on the path of your destiny.

| Low | 1 | 2 | 3 | 4 | 5 | 6 | 7 | 8 | 9 | 10 | High |
|-----|---|---|---|---|---|---|---|---|---|----|------|

# Chapter 7

## Manifestations of Brokenness

There are many ways that a broken heart is manifested in a person. I am going to list some of the ways that a satanic encounter, shattered dreams, broken hopes, shame and reproach can manifest after breaking the heart and spirit of a person.

Tick the box that highlights the persona that mirrors your experience when you are broken.

### 1. A depressed persona ☐
This manifestation of brokenness occurs when the causes of brokenness encourages a person to succumb to the spirit of heaviness and depression.

### 2. A frustrated persona ☐
This manifestation occurs when brokenness causes a person to develop dormant frustration when things do not turn out the way they would have liked. This frustration lies dormant in them like lava in a volcano and erupts periodically. It also affects them significantly when they are alone.

### 3. An angry persona ☐
This manifestation occurs when a person has dormant anger in them that erupts periodically like a volcano and negatively impacts the relationships they are closest to.

### 4. A confused person ☐
This manifestation occurs when brokenness causes a person to lose their moral compass and sense of direction in the area in which they were broken.

### 5. A bitter persona ☐
This occurs when the response to brokenness is unforgiveness which turns into emotional bitterness.

### 6. A withdrawn persona ☐
This occurs when a person's response to brokenness is to raise up emotional and mental walls of defense that they retreat behind. It stops people from getting intimate with them and stops them from getting intimate with people.

### 7. A reckless persona ☐
This manifestation occurs when a person throws all caution to the wind in the attempt to get some sort of emotional comfort in any place or form they can get it. This pursuit of comfort takes no account of the consequential actions.

### 8. An emotionally tired person ☐
This occurs when brokenness causes an emotional weariness which reduces your sense of pleasure in life.

## 9. A murderous persona ☐
In this manifestation, the response of a person is to seek to kill someone else's dream, character or life wrongly thinking it will ease some of the pain that they are feeling right now.

## 10. An envious persona ☐
In this manifestation, the person becomes bitter at anybody succeeding in the area where they experienced brokenness. For example, if their business dreams were shattered, they will begin to envy people who are succeeding in business, and if their marriage dreams were destroyed, they will envy people in good marriages.

## 11. A hateful person ☐
In this manifestation, people hate all things that remind them of their brokenness and expresses it in actions and words.

## 12. A defensive persona ☐
In this manifestation, people refuse to accept the truth about themselves if it is not flattering to them. To believe in it means that it will make them feel inferior and further weaken them after their experience of brokenness.

## 13. A suicidal persona ☐

This manifestation occurs when a person seeks to end his or her life so that they can end the pain caused by brokenness.

## 14. An emotionally immature persona ☐
This manifestation occurs when a person stays stuck mentally and emotionally in the moment of brokenness and cannot shake off those negative emotions in order to experience positive emotions.

## 15. A cowardly persona ☐
This manifestation occurs when brokenness leads people to run from any situation that causes negative emotions. This causes them to become a rolling stone that gathers very little to no moss in their relationships, careers and life.

## 16. A contentious persona ☐
This manifestation occurs when brokenness causes someone to fight everything and anyone that does not align with his or her views or actions.

## 17. A controlling persona ☐
This manifestation occurs when brokenness causes people to seek control over things they are not responsible for in their bid to avoid future pain.

## 18. An anxious persona ☐
This manifestation occurs when brokenness causes people to become fearful, anxious and have panic attacks about something the think is going to happen, like the previous brokenness that they may have experienced in their lives.

**19. An arrogant persona** ☐
This manifestation occurs when brokenness causes someone to overcompensate for the broken places in his or her life by appearing to know it all, have it all and have experienced it all.

**20. A crushed persona** ☐
This manifestation occurs when brokenness in a person causes their mind and body to shut down and become immobilized.


## PERSONAL APPLICATION

After ticking the relevant boxes, write out the ways in which brokenness has manifested itself through you.

_____

_____

_____

_____

_____

_____

_____

# Chapter 8

## LifeQuakes

An earthquake is defined as "a sudden and violent shaking of the ground, sometimes causing great destruction, as a result of movements within the earth's crust." One day when I was meditating on the subject of brokenness, the Holy Spirit ministered to me that while the earth experiences earthquakes of different magnitudes, people also experience life quakes of different magnitudes.

Earthquakes are more deadly than storms. Whilst a hurricane can blow your roof off and create tornadoes that can carry cars and trees many miles, they do not come from the ground up; they come from the sky downwards. Due to the fact that they come from the sky downwards, there are options to find places for shelter. However, with an earthquake there's no place to run because it's coming from the ground up and there is no shelter on the ground in an earthquake zone. This is similar to the storms of life and the earthquakes of life which I call "lifequakes".

I define a lifequake as a violent shaking and destruction of the foundational blocks on which a person's life is built upon. Lifequakes come in different categories and magnitudes.

An example of a relational lifequake is a nine year old child who loses both mother and father in a car accident and ends up in an orphanage. This child's daily existence was built on the relationship between his mother and father, and with that foundation violently taken from him, he's left with nothing but the effects of a lifequake of a very high magnitude. The intimacy between child and parents, the provision from parents to child, the protection from parents to child, the care etc, have all been violently destroyed. That nine year old boy has been broken in his heart by a lifequake.

Other examples of lifequakes are a shattering divorce, rape, untimely death of loved ones, bankruptcy, destruction of a home or business by a natural disaster, devastating sicknesses and diseases, a deadly betrayal or a false move that devastates the foundational blocks of your life etc.

Are lifequakes Unavoidable? They are not. Jesus in His time on the earth experienced several lifequakes and through the help of God was able to overcome them.

One of my favorite examples is found in *Luke 4: 28 -30* *"28 So all those in the synagogue, when they heard these things, were filled with wrath, and rose up and thrust Him out of the city; and they led Him to the brow of the hill on which their city was built, that they might throw Him down over the cliff. Then passing through the midst of them, He went His way...*

Lifequakes can be defined as situations that thrust you out of your place of peace and security and seek to throw you over the cliff of destruction. Jesus in this lifequake faced certain death but the anointing of the Holy Spirit, the angel of God, caused him to pass through the people and He overcome the lifequake.

To understand the emotional nature of this lifequake, it's important to know that Nazareth was Jesus' hometown; he knew them and they knew him and his family. It is a painful thing to be rejected by people however, it is more painful to be rejected by people you are anointed to help and who you know personally. These people did not only reject Him, they sought to kill Him for seeking to transform their lives with the anointing His Heavenly father had given Him. However, Jesus overcame and so will you overcome every lifequake that seeks to destroy your life and its foundation.

Some might ask what is the difference between the storms of life and the lifequakes of life? An example of a storm of life would be losing your car in an accident and walking away unscathed.

On the other hand, a lifequake would be getting injured in an accident and facing the loss of your limbs. A storm of life could also be a husband and wife having a season of disagreement and dissension.

A lifequake would be the two getting a divorce. A storm of life could be a parent and a child having terrible communication for a season, whereas a lifequake could be the child running away to another part of the world and disappearing off the parents' radar.

A storm of life could be not being able to pay your bills and having to live off the kindness of people for three years.

An example of a financial lifequake however, would be getting affected by an illness that causes you to lose your mental capacity to work and maintain yourself.
A storm of life could be thieves breaking into your home and stealing your furniture. A lifequake could be your hometown erupting into civil war with rape and executions being the order of the day.

Lifequakes and the storms of life both cause brokenness in people. However, lifequakes tend to be more devastating.

Let us now look at the different types of lifequakes:

## 1.  A False Move Lifequake

Life is made for movement and every major step you take will either lift you up, take you down or maintain the current status quo. It is impossible to sustain a quality of life that is greater than the quality of your decisions, choices and steps.

The book of proverbs states in Chapter 14;12 "...there is a way that seemeth right to a man but the end thereof is death...". This speaks to personal steps that people make that their emotions find appealing but creates devastation in the foundations of their lives and causes the good things that are in their lives to die.

Most people have something in life which works for them, be it spiritual, mental, emotional, physical, financial, relational or occupational. When you make a false move, even that which was adding value to your life, starts to die and may even be destroyed.

Samson made a choice to become sexually and emotionally intimate with Delilah and the consequence was the loss of his anointing, physical eyesight, personal freedom and an untimely death. Delilah in this context represents the embracing of an emotionally pleasing idea, person, venture, decision and step that will create foundational losses in your life.

Let us look at what Samson lost. He lost the mantle of the anointing of 'A Warrior Judge', which was at the foundation of his life and destiny. He also lost his eyesight, which is foundational for physical living, and then, his personal freedom and dignity by becoming a prisoner. He eventually paid the ultimate price and died before his time. May the Lord grant you the grace to avoid making a false move. There are lifequakes that occur in life that you cannot stop however, the false move is a self-inflicted lifequake that causes brokenness.

## 2. A Relational Lifequake

When God made man, He said in Genesis chapter *1:26* *"...let us make man in our own image and likeness..."*

The word us refers to the heavenly father, Jesus our Lord and the Holy Spirit.

Man was made by a relationship and therefore, man is relational in nature. Every human being operates with a team of people called us.

This us could be our parents, siblings, marriage spouses, boyfriends and girlfriends, fiancées, business partners or friends. When an unprepared termination of a relationship occurs that is part of the relational foundation of your life either through death, disloyalty, disagreement, desertion or disability, a lifequake is in progress. Relational lifequakes are very devastating and the nature of the relationship will determine the magnitude of the devastation. It is wisdom to take whatever steps possible within your power to avoid a relational lifequake.

## 3. Financial Lifequakes

Money is the fuel of your dreams. Its value in your life is the same as the value of petrol to a car. When a car runs out of petrol on its way to a destination, it creates a minor crisis. In the same token, when a person runs out of financial fuel for the basic dreams of life, which are food to eat or a house to sleep, they are on the way to experiencing a financial lifequake.

## 4. Spiritual Lifequake

This occurs when sin, the forces of darkness or both, have immobilized your life and are holding you hostage. Examples of spiritual lifequakes are people who have been immobilized by devastating curses, sins and oppression who stop the manifestation of their real identity and plunge them into a living hell.

## 5.  Physical Violence Lifequakes

These occur when people experience devastating physical violence such as assault, battery, rape, molestation and all of its psychological scars.

## 6.  Health Lifequakes

This occurs when your life and livelihood are threatened because of sickness, disease or infirmity.

## 7.  Mental and Emotional Lifequakes

This occurs when people suffer a mental and emotional breakdown.

## PERSONAL APPLICATION

List the type of lifequakes you have experienced in your life.

_____

_____

_____

_____

_____

_____

_____

_____

_____

_____

_____

# Chapter 9

## Broken In Many Places

The human body can be broken in multiple places and can become fragmented and disjointed. This is also the case with the human soul when the events of life break it multiple times. Without recovery from the past brokenness, fragmentation of the soul becomes the result.

When fragmentation of the soul takes place, the person develops more than two personas. I describe a persona as the way a person expresses his or her thoughts, feelings and opinions and the manner in which he or she acts. Let us take a deeper look at the subject. When people experience brokenness in their lives that remain unhealed, they can bury the situation in their emotional archives with all the negative emotions associated with that event and carry on life with their normal, natural persona.

There are three types of personas that a person is capable of having:

1. The first is their natural persona, which is the natural way they think, talk and act.
2. The second is the emotional wounded persona.
3. The third is the demonized persona.

When people are truly whole, they have only one persona, which is their natural persona. This is manifested in their daily lives. When a person has an unhealed broken heart caused by a single event, they have their natural persona as well as a secondary, emotional wounded persona. In the event of a negative circumstance or situation, the secondary, emotional wounded persona is triggered and becomes more dominant.

An example of this can be seen in the life of one of my staff members who managed one of my bank accounts and would not go to the bank's ATM to find out the balance on the account in order to provide me with a report. When I asked her why that was the case, she said that in the past she lived in so much poverty that she was fearful to check how much money was on the account in case there wasn't any. The thought of not having any money on the account triggered an anxiety attack which, caused her to write several bounced checks from her personal account. Although the business account had finances that she knew of, that persona was triggered whenever she approached an ATM machine.

In her natural persona, she was a likeable graduate in mass communication, television news reader and Jazz singer. She was fun, vivacious and interpersonal. She was also articulate, warm and very smart. However, when a situation such as going to the ATM machine to check the balance on the account was presented to her, she would become fearful, anxious and have a panic attack.

This was obviously irrational and when I asked her about it, she told me that during her days of poverty she would eat from the dustbins on the streets of New York. She lived in great surroundings and had no poverty issues at the time, yet this emotionally wounded poverty persona was lurking behind her natural persona waiting to be triggered. Her secondary persona was the anxiety of a child, afraid that she won't get a meal to eat. There are hundreds of personas that a person can have based on the circumstances of their brokenness.

I will now give you three examples of people I have encountered in my ministry with secondary personas. I have changed their names for confidentiality purposes. By God's grace, I have helped countless persons overcome brokenness in their lives on three continents so it is virtually impossible to know who I'm talking about.

## Case Study No. 1: A Withdrawn and Frustrated Persona

I shall start with myself. Growing up as a child, I had a severe stammer. It was so severe that I was unable to answer the telephone without the person on the other end getting angry and slamming down the receiver in my ears, often after a few choice words. This was because in my attempt to say hello, all they would hear was my heavy breathing.

This stammering was bad enough in a non-stressful environment but whenever I became stressed or troubled about a situation, I could not communicate a single word and tears of frustration would start coming out of my eyes. Under such circumstances, I would normally withdraw myself from people close to the situation and then act out of frustration in some way. When God healed me of the stammering, this secondary wounded persona was still unhealed and laid dormant, waiting to be triggered while my natural tranquil, warm, interpersonal, philosophical and dynamic persona ruled.

## Case Study No. 2: Contentious and Angry Persona

Karen grew up in a wealthy home. Her father was a man of high influence in the nation but was also a womanizer, alcoholic, moody and a very angry man When he was angry, he would take his guns, fire them in the air and scare his wife and children. He was so much of a player that he was having sex with schoolgirls. Karen later became born again and not very long after, a minister of the gospel. Even then, she still harbored deep anger against her father and one day physically attacked him. In her natural persona she was a joyful, prophetic and dynamic woman. However, in her secondary persona she was a woman who was contentious, angry and would not submit to any husband.

## Case study No. 3: - A Sexually Reckless Persona

John grew up in a family where his mother was a prostitute and his grandfather was a minister of the gospel who won thousands of people over to the Lord. As he grew up, he became a body builder and a personal trainer.

He was also exposed to pornography at the age of six and had developed a sexually reckless persona in his teen years. Thankfully, he became born again and managed to lead over two thousand people to Christ through personal evangelism. His natural persona was that of an interpersonal, dynamic, evangelistic soul winner. However, when stressed a sexual reckless persona was triggered for some light relief. This became a real bondage because he looked like a celebrity male model and was a fitness coach to ladies.


## People with Multiple Emotionally Wounded Personas

Things get complicated when people experience more than one devastating traumatic experience in their lives. When they are not healed of these experiences, more than two personas can develop. An example of this was a lady whom I will call Florence for confidentiality sake. In her natural persona she was confident, beautiful, articulate, sophisticated, intellectual and highly gifted. Her secondary personas were a sexually restlessness persona, a damsel in distress persona and a disenchanted persona.

1. She developed a sexually restlessness persona because her first husband held back from consummating the marriage for two years and was only intimate with her twice in five years.

2. She developed a damsel in distress persona because her second husband emptied one of her accounts of $50,000.00 and took off with his mistress whilst she was sick in hospital.

3.She had a disenchanted persona because one day, when she returned home from work, she found her second husband in her bra and panties.

These three secondary personas lay dormant and would only be manifested when triggered. In her daily life, she was a sweet giving, entrepreneurial millionaire. However, when triggered she will do things that could destroy what she represented.

The book of James 1:8 describes a double minded man as unstable in all his ways. One is primary and the other is secondary. Yet, there are some people who are not double minded and have multiple minds or personas.

## Demonized Personas

As I have stated earlier, you can have a person with a primary natural persona and multiple emotionally wounded personas. They require healing for their brokenness and not deliverance. Many people are of the mistaken perception that people with broken hearts always need deliverance.

Many do not, they simply need an encounter with the healing power of God. However, there are circumstances in which a person needs more than just the healing of wounded emotions, he or she needs deliverance because demons have attached themselves to the wounded persona.

In this case, a demonic bondage develops that requires the delivering power of God to destroy it. An example of this was a lady called Dianne. She had a wonderful, sweet, natural persona but she also had two secondary personas. One was emotionally depressing and the other was the emotionally bitter persona. She had experienced betrayal at the hands of a loved one.

Nevertheless, the depression and bitterness went beyond normal levels in and was powered by demon spirits. She was so depressed that she wouldn't have a bath for days partly because she was unable to get out of bed to carry out normal daily activities. She was set free of the depression only when the spirit of depression was cast out of her. Over the course of the months that followed, she overcame the bitterness and became whole again, totally free from both the bitterness and depression.

This can also be your story!

# Chapter 10

## The 5 Levels of Brokenness

*He healeth the broken in heart, and bindeth up their wounds (Psalm 147:3).*

In my studies on brokenness I have realized that there are five levels of intensity

1.  Emotional wounding
2.  A Broken Heart
3.  A fragmented Persona
4.  An Insane Persona
5.  A Suicidal Persona

## 1. <u>Emotional Wounding</u>

**An emotional wound is an unshakeable negative emotion rooted in a past circumstance that colors your response to present and future situations in the sphere of life the wound occurred.**

This occurs when situations create unhealed emotional wounds in specific areas of our soul. It causes pain but allows us to still function with an emotional limp and blurred vision in the sphere of life the wound occurred.

## 2.  A Broken Heart

**A broken heart is an unshakeable negative thought pattern and emotion, rooted in a past circumstance that prevents a person from functioning without crutches in the sphere of life the heart breaking circumstance occurred.**

This occurs when situations create unshakeable negative thought patterns and emotions rooted in a past circumstance, which hijacks the logic of the individual. This results in an inability to function in the sphere of life the heart breaking circumstance occurred without crutches.


## 3.  A Fragmented Persona

**A fragmented persona is multiple personality syndrome created by burying toxic emotions, unhealed wounds and a broken heart in the human psyche, in a bid to be courageous in the face of crushing emotional pain.**

This occurs when courageous people, in an attempt to navigate toxic emotions, unhealed wounds and a broken heart, unconsciously create different personas within themselves to function in certain spheres of life.


## 4.  An Insane Persona

**An insane persona is one that has surrendered to toxic emotions, unhealed wounds and a broken heart to such an extent, that it takes over and becomes the only reality he or she thinks, speaks and acts which renders a person unable to carry out his or her usual daily living responsibilities.**

This occurs when people give up on overcoming toxic emotions, unhealed wounds and a broken heart, and then retreat into the cave of despair which renders them unable to carry out their usual daily living responsibilities.

### 5. A Suicidal Persona

**A suicidal persona is one that has decided that the pain of premature, self-induced death is less than the pain of facing and overcoming toxic emotions, unhealed wounds and a broken heart.**

This occurs when people give up on overcoming toxic emotions, unhealed wounds and a broken heart and decide, based upon false assumptions, that the premature, self-induced death is less than the pain of living.

## PERSONAL APPLICATION

What is the highest level of brokenness you have experienced?

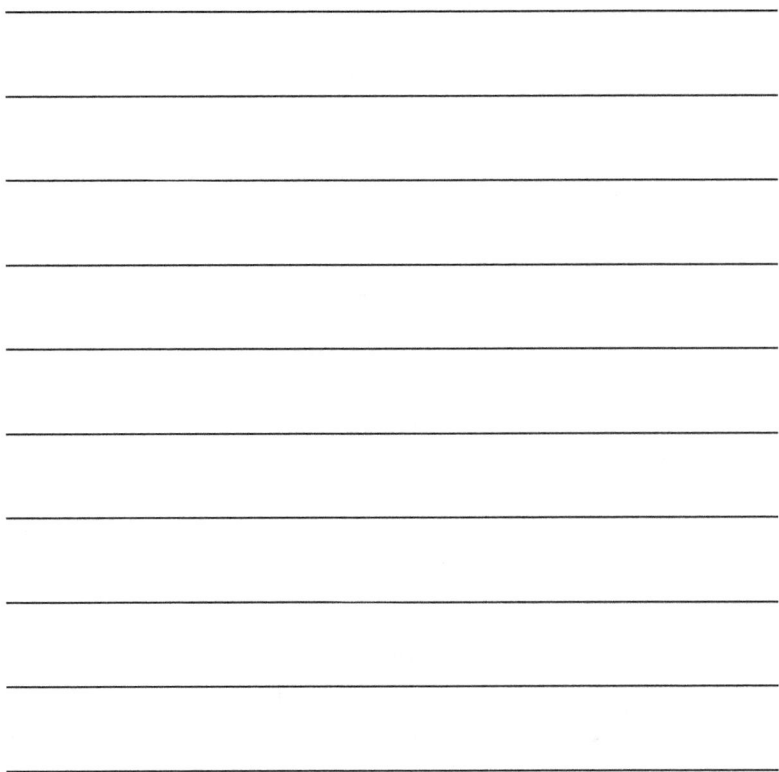

# Chapter 11

## The Road to Wholeness

*Psalm 51:6 "Behold, thou desirest truth in the inward parts and in the hidden parts: thou shall make me to know wisdom."*

The journey to wholeness requires:

1.  The right diagnosis of the cause and the nature of the brokenness. After he fell into adultery, David prayed that the Lord would make him know wisdom in the hidden parts of his life and experience truth in the inward parts of his life. He wanted to know the reason why he did what he did.

2.  An understanding of how brokenness has affected your persona and the habits it has created in you.

3.  An encounter with Jesus Christ, the Healer.

There are 4 types of encounters in the scriptures:

**A.  Personal Encounters**

This happens when you draw near to God privately through worship, prayer and fasting and He visits you with His presence and delivering power.

*In the first year of Darius the son of Ahasuerus, of the seed of the Medes, who was made king over the realm of the Chaldeans, in the first year of his reign, I, Daniel, understood the number of the years by books, which came of the Word of Jehovah to Jeremiah the prophet, that he would accomplish seventy years in the desolations of Jerusalem. And I set my face toward the Lord God, to seek by prayer and holy desires, with fasting, and sackcloth, and ashes. (Dan 9:1-3)And while I was speaking, and praying, and confessing my sin, and the sin of my people Israel, and presenting my cry before Jehovah my God for the holy mountain of my God; yes, while I was speaking in prayer, even the man Gabriel, whom I had seen in the vision at the beginning, touched me in my severe exhaustion, about the time of the evening sacrifice. And he enlightened me, and talked with me, and said, O Daniel, I have now come out to give you skill and understanding. At the beginning of your prayers the commandment came out, and I have come to explain. For you are greatly beloved; therefore understand the matter, and attend to the vision: (Dan 9:20-23)*

## B. A Divine Encounter through a Man or Woman of God

This occurs when a man or woman of God administrates an anointing from God that heals, delivers, empowers and gives you an encounter with the living God.

*And on the same day Peter and John went up into the temple at the hour of prayer, the ninth hour. And a certain man, who was lame from his mother's womb, was being carried. And they laid him daily at that temple gate which is called Beautiful, to ask alms from those who entered into the temple. Seeing Peter and John about to go into the temple, he asked to receive alms. And fastening his eyes on him, Peter with John said, Look on us! And he paid heed to them, expecting to receive something from them. But Peter said, Silver and gold have I none, but what I have I give you. In the name of Jesus Christ of Nazareth, rise up and walk! And taking him by the right hand, he lifted him up. And immediately his feet and ankle-bones received strength. And leaping up, he stood and walked and entered with them into the temple, walking and leaping and praising God. And all the people saw him walking and praising God. And they recognized him, that it was him who sat for alms at the Beautiful Gate of the temple. And they were filled with wonder and amazement at what had happened to him. And as the lame one who was healed held Peter and John, all the people ran together to them in the porch that is called Solomon's, greatly wondering. (Act 3:1-11)*

## C. A Corporate Anointing Encounter

This encounter occurs when the move of the Holy Spirit impacts a service like it did on the day of Pentecost and every one according to his hunger and faith receives a touch of God.

> And in the fulfilling of the day of Pentecost, they were all with one accord in one place. And suddenly a sound came out of the heaven as borne along by the rushing of a mighty wind, and it filled all the house where they were sitting. And tongues as of fire appeared to them, being distributed; and it sat upon each of them. And they were all filled of the Holy Spirit, and began to speak in other languages, as the Spirit gave them utterance. (Act 2:1-4)

## D. A Divine Sovereignty Encounter

This occurs when God in his sovereignty decides to move and heal and delver someone for his own purposes

> In the year that King Uzziah died I then saw the Lord sitting on a throne, high and lifted up, and His train filled the temple. Above it stood the seraphs; each one had six wings; with two he covered his face, and with two he covered his feet, and with two he flew. And one cried to another, and said, Holy, holy, holy, is Jehovah of Hosts; the whole earth full of His glory. And the doorposts moved at the voice of the one who cried, and the house was filled with smoke. Then I said, Woe is me! For I am undone; for I am a man of unclean lips, and I dwell in the midst of a people of unclean lips; for my eyes have seen the King, Jehovah

*of Hosts. Then one of the seraphs flew to me, having a live coal in his hand, snatched with tongs from the altar. And he laid it on my mouth and said, Lo, this has touched your lips; and your iniquity is taken away, and your sin purged. And I heard the voice of the Lord, saying, Whom shall I send, and who will go for us? Then I said, Here am I; send me! And He said, Go, and tell this people, You hear indeed, but do not understand; and seeing you see, but do not know. (Isa 6:1-9)*

∅ **Focus on discovering yourself and manifest your authentic self in all spheres of your life.**

∅ **Disconnect from all human and medical emotional crutches and intentionally build wonderful life giving relationships.**

∅ **Study and embrace God's pattern and principles as you pursue your life's mission with all your heart.**

In all four seasons of brokenness in my life I was healed by a divine encounter through a man of God. In the fifth season I was healed by an intervention of divine sovereignty.

# Greatness Publishing

**BOOKS BY NINA THOMAS**

Woman, Get off that Bus

**OTHER BOOKS BY ANDRE THOMAS**

Discovering Me
The Gift of Political Leadership
The Gift of Organizational Leadership
Unlock your Greatness
(A Young Leaders Handbook)
Uncommon Men and Distinguished Women
(A Rites of Passage Manual)

## FRESH ANOINTING & WISDOM NETWORK

# Tours

**BISHOP**
**Andre**
**& Nina**
**PROPHETESS**
**THOMAS**

**THE BONDAGE TO GREATNESS TOUR**
This tour centers on activating greatness in people, delivering people from bondages and bringing healing to the broken and afflicted.

**THE ANOINTING FOR LEADERSHIP TOUR**
This tour centers on empowering Gods people to become influencers and bring transformation to their nation.

**THE WOMAN, GET OFF THAT BUS TOUR**
This tour centers on empowering woman to overcome life's challenges and provide fuel for their journey of self-discovery and greatness.

**ECONOMIC IDEAS AND SOLUTIONS TOUR**
This tour centers on divinely empowering people to take entrepreneurial ideas from concept to reality and rescue economies from ruin.

To book Bishop Andre & Prophetess Nina Thomas and host one of these tours in your city or nation:

Email: cool@ideasandsolutions.org or visit
Website: http://www.anointingandwisdom.org

To view Bishop Andre Thomas books go to
http://www.amazon.com/author/andrethomas

62

# ABOUT THE 12 LEADER MOVEMENT

### PURPOSE
To raise up a global movement of The 12 Types of Leaders that Shape the Destinies of Nations.

### VISION
To see a movement of The 12 Types of Leaders serve Heavenly solutions that shape the destinies of nations.

### MISSION
To raise up a global movement of The 12 Types of Leaders that Shape the Destinies of Nations through events, partnerships, networking resources and online training.

### OUR INVITATION
We invite you to become a part of this movement that will unlock your greatness by reading our resources and applying the principles, subscribing to our digital newsletter, hosting an event, attending one of our extension campuses or hosting an extension campus.

**How can my church, town, city or nation be transformed by the 12 Leaders Movement?**

There are 3 different events that Andre and Nina Thomas may be booked for:

## 1. Anointing for Leadership Annual Conference

This is our most comprehensive conference running for 3-4 days. Andre and Nina Thomas will minister in detail on The 12 Spheres of Leadership and also hold Anointing and Prayer sessions to activate people into their leadership callings.

## 2. Leadership Sphere Seminar

This seminar runs for 1-3 days depending on the needs of the host. Andre and Nina Thomas will focus on one particular sphere of leadership, chosen by the host. This seminar can cater to faith-based audiences or secular audiences.

*Customized workbooks will be available for purchase.

## 3. Andre and Nina Thomas are also available for speaking engagements at events that deal with any of the topics covered in the 12 Leaders curriculum.

www.ingramcontent.com/pod-product-compliance
Lightning Source LLC
Chambersburg PA
CBHW071632040426
42452CB00009B/1586